NOT YOUR DAD'S ACCOUNTING

FINANCIAL CLARITY FOR THE NEW GENERATION

BY KELLY COUGHLIN, CPA AND CAT GLASS, CPA

EVERYDAYCPA, INC.

First Edition — 2026

DEDICATION

This book is dedicated to my great-great-grandfather, Laurence Coughlin, and to my eldest brother, Michael Coughlin.

Laurence left the coal mines of Pennsylvania in the early 1900s and made his way to Galveston, Texas, where he worked as a junior accountant for the Atchison, Topeka & Santa Fe Railroad. Galveston was still recovering from the devastating Hurricane of 1900, a storm that reshaped the city and tested the resilience of everyone who lived there.

In a world that had been thrown into chaos, Laurence helped bring order — one journal entry at a time. In doing so, he laid the tracks for future generations, including my brother Michael and me, to become CPAs.

Michael Coughlin, my eldest brother by twelve years, also laid tracks for our family. In a household of ten, he influenced all of us through chess, music, discipline, intellect, and, yes, accounting.

Mike was on his way to becoming one of those exceptionally bright math and physics academics, working toward his PhD in Physics at Ohio State University. As he neared completion, President John F. Kennedy's call to reach the moon was still inspiring many young scientists and engineers. But Michael looked at that future and realized that spending his career surrounded by "Einsteins" was not really his thing.

So he pivoted to business — specifically, to accounting.

He earned his MBA and CPA in record time and began his career with one of the top accounting firms in the country in what is now known as Silicon Valley. He later returned to the Midwest, where he built and operated his own CPA firm.

More importantly, he became a lasting influence on me — through his business insight, precision, discipline, and guidance.

For these two, and others, I am deeply grateful.

TABLE OF CONTENTS

FOREWORD

I have been an accountant for 31 years. Started by hand, moved to spreadsheets, Lotus, Excel, and every version of QuickBooks ever shipped. I've sat across from truck drivers, software founders, hair stylists, creators, and business owners of every kind and tried to explain why their books don't match their bank accounts. I know the look on their faces.

That look is one of frustration, confusion, and sometimes embarrassment. Not because they are careless. Not because they are bad business owners. But because the system was never really designed for them.

When Cat and I began trying to understand why business owners were having so much friction and difficulty getting their "numbers" to us, we started looking for the root cause. That search became the genesis of this book.

This book is about a very old system — more than 500 years old — that still works but is frankly outdated and inefficient for business owners in today's world of advanced machine learning, artificial intelligence, and metadata.

The old paradigm says every transaction must have a debit and a credit. That system was brilliant in its time. It created order, discipline, and accountability.

The old system still works but that does not mean business owners should be forced to run it. But for decades, this is all our industry has offered: a double-entry accounting system and the tasks that come with it— bank feeds, categorizations, credit card reconciliations, journal entries, charts of accounts, and financial statements most owners do not fully understand.

This book is not about promoting one specific replacement system.

It's about why a new system is required.

The old system was created for a class of trained workers charged with counting, measuring, and reporting transactions for merchants and rulers. But for modern business owners who attempt to use it and fail, the system becomes worthless. The current system is a half-baked cake. The ingredients may be right. The recipe may be proven. But unless the cake is fully baked, nobody wants to eat it.

The system only works if it is operated correctly. And most business owners are not accountants.

We continue to design systems around accounting work instead of business owner outcomes. We ask customers to adapt to our process. We expect non-accountants to use accountant-centered tools. And then, when they fail to keep up, we act surprised.

The purpose of this book is to reverse our approach.

In *Not Your Dad's Accounting: Financial Clarity for a New Generation*, we are asking CPAs, accountants, bookkeepers, and software companies to look at accounting from the customer's side of the table.

The question should not begin with: How do we get the business owner to think like an accountant? The better question is: What does the business owner really need to know about their business?

If we want to build better accounting firms, better products, and better financial systems for businesses, we must stop forcing owners to think like accountants.

We must start designing accounting around the needs and decision-making realities of the people we claim to serve. That is the shift this book is trying to make.

Once you see that distinction, the question changes. It stops being, "How do we train more business owners to keep up with accounting?" and becomes, "Why are we still asking them to do this in the first place?"

It is time for business owners to spend more time running their business and less time learning and doing accounting.

— Kelly Coughlin, CPA

CEO, EverydayCPA, Inc.

ABOUT THE AUTHOR

Kelly Coughlin is a Certified Public Accountant (CPA), business strategist, and entrepreneur with more than three decades of experience helping business owners make better financial decisions.

He is the founder and CEO of EverydayCPA, Inc., a tax and accounting firm established in 2012 to serve business owners who need more than compliance—they need clarity.

Kelly's work focuses on simplifying the complex world of accounting, taxes, and financial systems. He has helped hundreds of households and businesses navigate financial uncertainty by turning confusing information into practical, decision-ready insight.

He earned his MBA from Babson College and studied accounting at the University of Minnesota. His academic journey began in classical history at Gonzaga University, where he studied Greek and Roman civilizations, and later expanded into Russian studies at the Middlebury Institute of International Studies.

Kelly draws heavily from history in both his thinking and writing. He credits many of history's great thinkers as informal mentors, including Sun Tzu, Aristotle, Julius Caesar, and Luca Pacioli. He also considers Michael Porter's Five Forces framework a defining influence on his understanding of competition and strategy.

He comes from a family with four generations of accountants and still believes in the power of structured financial systems—but also recognizes their limitations in a modern world.

This book reflects that tension.

ABOUT THE AUTHOR

Cat Glass, CPA, CFF, CVA is the President and Creative Director of Creator's Consultant and serves as VP of Marketing at EverydayCPA, Inc. and ECPA ProServices, Inc. She's known for making the conversation around money and taxes feel less intimidating—and a lot more human.

Cat spent over a decade in corporate technology and helped launch fintech products like QuickBooks Live and Mint Live, giving her a deep understanding of how people actually use financial tools in real life.

She graduated from Birmingham Southern College and spent seven years in forensic accounting, specializing in financial investigations.

At 35, Cat left the corporate world to build her own company, focused on helping women entrepreneurs keep more of their money and build wealth—all on their own terms.

Based in Alabama, Cat balances her professional life with time outdoors. When she is not working, she can be found at the beach, on a snowboard, or with her animals—a dog, a horse, and a hairless cat.

INTRODUCTION

I come from four generations of accountants. That probably explains more than I'd like to admit. My family is Irish and German. The Irish side gave me a love for people, storytelling, and a certain comfort in chaos. The German side gave me something else entirely— a need for order.

There's a particular satisfaction that comes from a system where everything has a place. Where every transaction is accounted for. Where nothing is left unresolved.

In accounting, every transaction has two sides. A debit. A credit. You don't get to ignore one. You don't get to delete the inconvenient parts. It's not like your email inbox, where you can delete 90% of what comes in and pretend it never existed.

In accounting, when something comes in, you must deal with it. You must define it. You must place it somewhere. Because if you don't— the system breaks. The books fall out of balance.

Maybe that's why accountants like me are drawn to it. Not just for the certainty. But for the illusion that if the books balance, maybe everything else does too.

This mindset goes back generations in my family. My great-great-grandfather, Larence Coughlin, started as a junior accountant on the railroad. He audited rolling stock moving across the country—tracking assets, reconciling movement, bringing structure to something that never stopped moving. And like a lot of railroad families, the job stayed in the family and passed down to his sons and grandsons.

Accounting wasn't just a profession. It was a path. I followed that path. But I didn't start in an office. During the summers, I worked on the railroad. In the sweltering, humid, breezeless Kansas summer air. It was hard. Hot. Relentless. And it taught me something I've never forgotten.

There are easier ways to make a living. That experience pulled me towards accounting. Toward a profession where the work was structured. Predictable. Controlled.

Our clients may not care about debits and credits. They may not understand adjusting entries or closing entries. But they understand the burden. They understand the emails asking for missing information. They understand the receipts they forgot to save, the categories they guessed at, the bank feeds they ignored, and the tax deadline that always seems to arrive before the records are ready.

For a long time, the old way of accounting worked. Until it didn't. And for many businesses, that is what this book is about. That is who this book is written for.

HOW TO READ THIS BOOK

If you are a business owner, you did not buy this to spend a weekend on it. If you are a CPA, you already know most of what is in the first few chapters — you're here for what comes after.

The first few chapters are historical. Pacioli, clay tablets, the railroad, the merchant. If you already accept that double-entry accounting works and that most people using it today aren't trained to use it, skim those chapters. The story is there for the reader who needs it. You may not be that reader.

The middle chapters are the argument. What the system requires, why the business owner isn't equipped to deliver it, and what happens when the system stops depending on the business owner. If you read nothing else, read this.

The last chapters are about what happens next. The economics. The firms that will adapt and the ones that won't. At the end there is a short section on what you might actually do on Monday morning — separated by whether you're a business owner or an accounting professional.

There is a glossary at the back. We assume you know a few accounting terms. We assume you do not know all of them, and that is fine.

One last thing.

If at some point you find yourself annoyed by something we've written, stay with it a page or two longer. Most of the real arguments in accounting happen in the paragraph after the one that bothered you.

BEFORE YOU BEGIN

WHERE DO YOU STAND?

Below are twelve statements. Read each one and answer whether it describes you right now.

- ☐ I know what my business made last month, before expenses and after.
- ☐ I reconcile my bank accounts on a schedule — the same day each month, or close to it.
- ☐ When a transaction appears in my bookkeeping software that I do not recognize, I resolve it within a week.
- ☐ I can tell you which of my products or services is most profitable without calling someone.
- ☐ I have not had a year-end "cleanup" fee from my CPA in the last two years.
- ☐ My business expenses and personal expenses are on different cards.

- ☐ If I needed to apply for a loan tomorrow, I could produce current, accurate financial statements by the end of the week.
- ☐ I spend less than two hours a week on anything that could be called bookkeeping.
- ☐ When I look at last month's P&L, I understand every line on it.
- ☐ I have, at some point in the last 6 months, made a decision about my business because of something I saw in my financial statements.
- ☐ Getting my "numbers" ready for tax season is easy.
- ☐ When I file my tax return, the tax due is not a surprise.

If you answered yes to 9 or more, you are in the small minority of business owners. You do not need this book. You are welcome to read it anyway, but what follows is mostly a confirmation of things you already suspect.

If you answered yes to 5 or more but fewer than 9, you are like most readers of this book. You are not failing at accounting. You are doing it in the margins of a life that is already busy enough. The chapters ahead were written for you.

If you answered yes to fewer than 5, you are not alone. This is how the system is actually used — by people who have other things to do and no real way to keep up. Read on.

CHAPTER 1

FROM CLAY TABLETS TO LEDGERS

There was a time when accounting did not exist. Not because people didn't need it. But because they hadn't yet figured out how to do it yet.

Long before spreadsheets, software, ledgers and journals, there was a much simpler problem:

How do you keep track of what you have and what you owe? It sounds like a small question. The earliest attempts to answer it appeared in ancient civilizations—places where trade was growing, resources were being managed, and someone, somewhere, needed to know whether things were going well. In regions that would later become part of modern-day Iran and Iraq, early societies began recording transactions on clay tablets.

These were not financial statements in the modern sense. There were no income summaries, balance sheets, or year-end reports. There were marks. Symbols. Impressions pressed into clay. Grain received. Livestock counted. Goods exchanged. It was less "accounting" and more "don't forget what just happened." Which, to be fair, is still a large part of accounting today.

In ancient Egypt, the need for recordkeeping expanded as the scale of society grew. Agriculture, labor, and taxation required coordination, and coordination required tracking. Officials documented harvests. They tracked storage. They recorded distributions.

If the Nile flooded at the right time, things went well. If it didn't, the records became very important, very quickly. Accounting, at this stage, was not about optimization or planning. It was about survival. As trade expanded across regions, systems became more structured. Commerce was no longer local. It moved. And when things move, they need to be accounted for. But for all their usefulness, these early systems shared a limitation.

They could record activity, but they could not guarantee accuracy. If a number was wrong, it stayed wrong—until someone noticed. And noticing required either exceptional memory or suspicion. Neither of which scales particularly well. For centuries, this limitation remained.

Over time, records improved. Methods became more organized. But the underlying challenge persisted: How do you know the records are correct? That question would eventually be answered in a more structured way by Luca Pacioli. Pacioli did not invent accounting. He did something more important. He organized it. In the late 15th century, Pacioli documented a system that would become the foundation of modern accounting: double-entry. At its core was a simple but powerful idea:

Every transaction has two sides. What you receive and how you got it. If you record both sides and they are expected to balance, something interesting happens. Errors become visible. This was the breakthrough.

Double-entry accounting created a system that could verify itself. If something didn't balance, something was wrong. And while that may seem obvious now, at the time it was revolutionary. It turned accounting from a recordkeeping exercise into a system of validation.

Of course, there was a catch. For the system to work, someone had to record every transaction; understand what was being recorded; classify it correctly; maintain consistency; check the work. In other words, the system required discipline. Not occasional discipline. Constant discipline.

And for centuries, that was acceptable. Because the people using the system were not casual participants. They were trained. They were bookkeepers, merchants, and financial stewards who understood the rules and respected the structure. Accounting was not something everyone did. It was something certain people were responsible for. And when it was done well, it worked beautifully. Records were organized. Balances were maintained. Information could be trusted.

But it is important to understand why it worked. It worked because the person using it knew how to use it. This caveat would become increasingly important as the system evolved. Because as accounting moved forward—into ledgers, firms, and eventually into software—something subtle began to change. The system remained the same. But the person using it had changed.

Accounting did not begin as a convenience. It began as a necessity. It evolved because the world became more complex, and it worked because the people responsible for it were equipped to handle that complexity. But that raises a question that would not have mattered centuries ago—and now matters more than ever:

What happens when the system stays the same but the user does not?

CHAPTER 2

EVERY TRANSACTION HAS TWO SIDES

The farmer had a problem. He kept records. Simple ones. Marks, notes, small reminders of what had happened—what he traded, what he received, and what he was owed. It was better than relying on memory. But it wasn't enough. One season, he traded grain for tools. He wrote it down. "Tools received." That seemed sufficient.

Weeks later, he tried to make sense of what he wrote. He looked at his notes. "Tools received. Grain harvested. Livestock counted."

But something was missing. Not from the list, but from his understanding. Because while he had recorded what he received, he had not fully captured what it cost him. This was the limitation of early recordkeeping. It captured activity. But not structure.

The farmer knew he had tools. But how much grain had he given up? Was it worth it? What did he have left? The answers were not obvious. Because he had only recorded one side of the transaction. And one side, it turns out, is not enough.

Enter the merchant. The merchant faced the same problem—but more often, and with greater consequences. He sold goods daily. Some customers paid immediately. Others promised to pay later. He bought inventory on credit. He paid suppliers when he could. At the end of the week, he reviewed his records. Sales were listed. Payments were listed. Purchases were listed.

And yet, he still could not answer a simple question with confidence:

Where do I stand? Because, like the farmer, he had recorded pieces of transactions—but not the full structure of them. He knew what had happened. But not how it all fit together.

Every transaction has two sides. Not one. Two. If you receive something, you must also have given up something. If the farmer receives tools, he gives up grain. If the merchant sells goods, he gives up inventory and receives money—or the promise of it.

This idea—as simple as it sounds—is the foundation of double-entry accounting.

Debits describe what you received. This side of the transaction answers a straightforward question: What did you get? If you buy a car, you received a car. If you buy a printer, you received equipment. But even here, something subtle happens. Not everything you receive is the same. Some things are used quickly and disappear within weeks or months. These are expenses.

Others last longer than a year and provide value over time. These are assets or the things you own that are worth money. Both your car and printer are assets. But they are treated differently from expenses. Both are debits, because they represent what you gained—but they also require judgment about how long that gain lasts. And that judgment matters.

Credits describe how you received it. What did you give up for the car or printer? Did you give up cash? Did you use your credit card? Did you borrow from a bank? All of these explain how you were able to get the asset you are buying.

You've probably heard the term "balance sheet." Well, this is where the balance occurs. Every debit, asset, and expense must have an explanation for how it got there. If funds were borrowed, the credit is a liability. If it was an investment in exchange for ownership in the company, it is equity. Total assets (the things you got) must equal what you gave up.

If you gave up your services or goods and exchanged them for another's goods or services, both of you would debit and credit the same transaction. You would debit the goods/services you received, and credit what you gave up.

Credits explain the source. Debits explain the result. And both must be recorded. If you are confused about this explanation of double entry, you are not alone.

For every transaction, the business owner must identify what was received, decide how to classify it, determine how it was paid for, and record both sides correctly and consistently. Not once. Every single time.

The farmer, the merchant, the yachtie, the creator, all must decide: Is this an expense or an asset? Is this a liability or equity? Is this new money in my account—income, loan, or a transfer of money? This is not a mechanical task. They are judgment calls. And the system depends on those judgments being made consistently.

Fast forward centuries later, this structure remains the same. Only the tools have changed. Modern systems—like QuickBooks—still require the same decisions.

Only now, instead of writing in a journal, the user clicks a dropdown, selects a category, and approves/clears a transaction. The process feels easier. But the responsibility is still there. Every click is still a decision. And if that decision is wrong, the system reflects it.

The realization is that most people do not think this way. They don't think about what a debit versus a credit is. Instead, they think, "I bought something" or "I paid someone." However, the double-entry system requires non-accountants to classify these events like accountants. This is where things break down.

Double-entry accounting is not flawed. It is precise. Logical. Proven. But it was designed for a world where trained individuals performed the work. Today, the system is used by people who are not trained accountants, do not have the time, and do not think in accounting terms.

And yet, the expectation remains.

The system is not complicated because it is flawed. It is not flawed. It is complicated because it requires judgment—over and over again. And for the system to work, those judgments must be made consistently every time. But who really should be expected to make them?

CHAPTER 3

THE CREATOR

She earns her money in ways her parents can't explain to their friends.

A subscription platform pays her on the 5th of every month. A second pays her on the 20th. She sells a digital workbook on another platform, which takes a cut and remits the rest 60 days later. She films content twice a month for a skincare company that sometimes pays late. She accepts tips.

Her mother, a retired schoolteacher, once asked what she did for a living. She tried to explain. Her mother nodded politely and changed the subject. The accounting is more complicated than the explanation.

She spends money on video equipment, travel, subscriptions and personal expenses that may or may not be business-related. The volume of transactions is not small. It is constant. And unlike the merchant, she does not end her day by sitting down with a journal. She moves on to the next thing.

At the end of the week, she may glance at her bank account. At the end of the month, she might log into a system. At the end of the year, she feels it. Because the system is still there. Waiting.

Every transaction still needs to be categorized. Not because she wants to do it. But because the system requires it. So, she does what most people do. She postpones. "I'll do it later."

Later becomes next week, next month, next tax season. When tax season arrives, she does what most creators do. She finds the cheapest bookkeeper online. But the work is no longer maintenance. It is reconstruction. Transactions are reviewed for the first time. Categories are guessed. Errors are corrected. Information is rebuilt. The system that was supposed to run continuously is rebuilt in a hurry.

And this comes at a cost. Time. Money. Back-and-forth communication. And even then, the result is often "good enough." This pattern is not unique to creators.

A year ago, she made the switch. The transactions are still chaotic. But now her bookkeeping system keeps up with her. Every transaction is classified before she sees it. A weekly summary arrives in her inbox every Monday morning. She spends ten minutes a week reviewing her finances.

Twelve months later, she has not missed a single Monday review. This is the most consistent she has been about her finances in the last seven years. What she wanted was numbers she could trust, on the Monday of any given week, that told her what she had made, what she had spent, and how much she had left.

She never wanted to be an accountant.

CHAPTER 4

ACCOUNTING ISN'T THE PROBLEM—DOING IT IS

Let's be clear about something. Accounting is not broken. It is one of the most reliable systems ever created. It is logical. It is structured. It has worked for over five hundred years. If you follow the rules, it works. Every time.

So, when business owners struggle with accounting, the natural assumption is: They're doing something wrong. They need more training. More discipline. More consistency. This assumption is everywhere. And it is wrong.

Take a contractor. He works long hours. He signs up for QuickBooks because he is told it will keep him organized. It will give him visibility. It will help him stay on top of things. And at first, it looks like it will. The dashboard lights up. Transactions start flowing in automatically. Income is there. Expenses are there. It feels like control. Until it isn't.

The industry keeps asking. How do we make accounting easier? How do we train business owners? Wrong questions. The real question is: Why are we still asking people to do this at all?

Because if a process only works when everyone follows it correctly (and most people don't), the failure isn't in the people using it. The failure is in the design.

Accounting isn't the problem. It never was. The problem is expecting millions of people to think like accountants or act like bookkeepers. And then being surprised when it doesn't work. The system works perfectly. But only for the people it was designed for.

Everyone else? They're just trying to survive it. And once you see that clearly, the next step becomes obvious. Not better tools. Not better training. A different approach entirely. Because the real solution isn't helping people do accounting better. It's removing the need for them to do it at all.

CHAPTER 5

A WORLD WITHOUT ACCOUNTING

Imagine waking up and not thinking about your books. Not because you forgot. Not because you're behind. Because there's nothing to catch up on. No transactions waiting. No categories to assign. No missed calls from your CPA.

For most people running a business, this doesn't feel realistic. Because their experience has taught them something very different. You don't think about accounting all the time. But it's always there. In the background.

You feel it when you swipe your card and wonder how you'll categorize it later. It's not overwhelming every moment. But it never fully goes away. And when it does show up, it shows up all at once.

You tell yourself: "I'll get to it." Later. This weekend. Next week. And you mean it.

But life doesn't slow down. Work doesn't stop. So the system waits. And the longer it waits, the heavier it feels. It's a quiet frustration no one talks about. Because it feels like something you should have figured out by now. Everyone else seems to be "on top of it." But here's the truth:

They're not. They're just better at hiding it. Or they're paying someone else to deal with it. Or they're ignoring it, just like you. Every tax season, everything you pushed aside comes back. All at once. Now it matters. Now it's urgent. Now it's stressful. You gather documents. You answer questions. You try to remember what happened months ago.

And somewhere in the process, you think: "There has to be a better way than this." But the system doesn't offer one. It just resets the clock.

It doesn't matter who you are. A contractor working twelve hour days. A creator with income coming from five different platforms. A W-2 employee trying to build something on the side. Different lives. Different income. Different complexity. Same issue.

Now imagine something different. You open your phone. And instead of work waiting for you...

There's an answer. Clear. Current. Complete. You don't wonder if it's right. You don't need to fix it. You don't need to "get caught up." It's just there. You don't prepare for tax season. You're already prepared. You don't guess at your numbers. You trust them. You don't avoid the system. Because there's nothing to avoid.

The biggest change isn't technical. It's emotional. You go from behind and unsure to current and confident. A world without accounting doesn't mean a world without financial clarity. It means a world where financial clarity comes easily, without requiring business owners to learn accounting just to run their business.

CHAPTER 6

THE NEW MODEL

What replaces manual accounting? Removing the work is one thing. Replacing it with something that functions—consistently and accurately is another.

Start With the Outcome, Not the Process

Traditional accounting starts with activity. Enter transactions. Categorize them. Reconcile accounts. Produce reports. Why not reverse this?

Instead, start with the outcome. What does the business owner need to know? What decisions do they need to make? What information actually matters? Everything else is built backward from that. The goal is not to maintain books. It's to deliver clarity so the business owner can keep more of what they earn.

Data Already Exists—Stop Recreating It

In the old model, the business owner creates the data. In the new model, the data already exists. Every transaction today is generated digitally and stored within an application. The problem is not the lack of data. It's what happens next.

Traditionally, the business owner reviews and categorizes it. What if we could eliminate this step? Instead, the new system ingests the raw financial data and takes responsibility for what happens next, instead of relying on the business owner.

You Don't Need to Learn Accounting

This is where traditional systems break down. They ask the business owner:

"What is this?" And the business owner guesses.

The new system would integrate historical patterns, behavioral mapping, and rule-based logic enhanced by AI. Each transaction is evaluated and assigned a purpose. Not based on one decision. But based on a system that learns, adjusts, and improves over time. Consistency is no longer dependent on the business owner learning accounting.

Embedded Double-Entry

This is the part that matters most. Double-entry accounting is not eliminated. It is embedded. The difference is simple. The business owner never sees it. They don't choose debits, assign credits, or manage accounts. The system does. Continuously. Accurately. Without exception. The new system affords the business owner the luxury of never lifting a finger.

Continuous Reconciliation

In traditional systems, reconciliation is an activity the business does, or fails to do, every month. This ensures company bank and credit card balances match the statements. And if they do not, there is an explanation for this imbalance. It is an annoying, manual process that requires human intervention. All reporting, if expected to be accurate, is delayed until this is completed.

Reconciliation should not be a task for the business owner to complete. In the new model, transactions are captured at the source. Balances are validated continuously. Discrepancies are identified immediately. There is no backlog. There is no "catching up." The system is not cleaned up. It is kept clean.

More Than a Fancy Report

This is where most systems stop. They produce reports. But the value isn't the fancy report. It's the insights the business owner uses to make decisions. The whole point of owning a business is to make money. These decisions directly affect future revenues, cost savings and ultimately how much the business owner gets to keep.

The whole point of reporting is to know where your money is going, how the business is performing, and what you should do next. Not in accounting jargon, but in a language everyone can understand. The new model speaks to the business owner.

Another weakness of today's traditional accounting systems is that they are usually built around the legal entity, not the owner. This works reasonably well when a person owns one business and uses one bank account. But many business owners do not live this way.

Traditional double-entry usually requires each business to maintain its own separate general ledger. The owner's personal financial life is treated separately. The spouse's financial life may be separate again. Then, if the owner wants to understand the full picture, someone has to manually combine, adjust, eliminate, and interpret all of this information.

This is difficult for accountants.

It is nearly impossible for most business owners.

The problem is that traditional accounting systems are not designed to answer the owner's most important question: "What is my total financial picture?"

Instead, they answer narrower questions:

"Did my LLC make money this year?" "How did my corporation perform?" "What does this one set of books show?" These are useful questions, but they are not enough.

An owner may need to see all companies together. Or only some companies. Or only the LLCs. Or only the business that pays estimated tax payments. Or personal activity combined with business activity to understand total cash flow.

The ability to look at more than one business at a time matters because estimated tax payments, cash flow planning, debt capacity, investment decisions, and wealth-building decisions are often driven by the owner's combined economic reality—not by one isolated general ledger.

Traditional accounting is entity centered. But true financial clarity is owner centered. This is one of the biggest differences between an accounting system designed to record history and a system designed to help owners make better business decisions.

10 Minute Reviews

In the new system, the owner does very little. Instead of maintaining the system, the owner is only interacting with exceptions. And this shouldn't require more than 10 minutes a week.

If something is unclear, the system flags it. If something needs confirmation, the system requests it. Otherwise? The system runs. The business owner is no longer the operator.

Built for Imperfect Behavior

This may be the most important difference. Traditional systems assume consistency and disciplined engagement. The new model assumes the opposite. Business owners are busy. They forget and are inconsistent. And it works anyway. Because it does not depend on the business owner's behavior.

Integration With Professional Oversight

The new model does not eliminate the accountant. It elevates them. Instead of fixing books, correcting errors, and reconstructing records, they can provide even more value. They can focus on planning, advising, and saving their clients' money.

When the business owner has accurate, complete, and organized financial information from the beginning, the accountant can move up the value chain. Instead of spending the client's budget cleaning up the past, the accountant can help shape the future.

They can evaluate operating ratios, identify trends, interpret profit margins, and help owners understand what the numbers are really saying. They can advise on pricing, staffing, cash flow, financing, digital marketing spend, return on investment, mergers, acquisitions, and growth decisions.

A good accountant is not merely someone who records what happened. A good accountant is trained to see what the numbers mean. And when the numbers are accurate, organized, and available, that accountant can help the business owner make better decisions about pricing, hiring, borrowing, investing, marketing, and taxes.

In other words, the accountant becomes less of a repair technician and more of a strategic advisor. This is the real promise of the new model. It does not reduce the accountant's importance. It removes the low-value friction that has consumed the accountant's time and the client's money.

When the accounting process no longer burns through the budget just to produce a usable set of books, that same budget can be redirected toward higher-value services that actually help the business owner make better decisions, reduce taxes, improve profits, and build long-term wealth.

CHAPTER 7

THE TRUCKER

He runs two trucks out of a terminal east of Dallas. Ten years in. His wife handles the dispatching. He does the driving and until eighteen months ago, his own version of bookkeeping.

His version is a shoebox with receipts in it. A thumb-torn spiral notebook. A login to software he uses only four times a year.

He is not a bad business owner. He is not lazy. He is not irresponsible. He is a trucker. He spends his time driving, hauling, loading, unloading, maintaining equipment, dealing with brokers, watching fuel prices, and trying to keep the truck moving.

Accounting is not his trade. Trucking is. But the system treats him as if he should also be a part-time bookkeeper.

Every April, he is supposed to hand everything over to his CPA. But every April, he explains he isn't ready. So, he files an extension.

He is finally ready by September. By then, his CPA is faced with the task of sorting through incomplete information, inconsistent records, questionable categories, missing explanations, and numbers that may or may not tie to anything. The preparer has to charge an additional $500 because the records are a mess.

The CPA works earnestly to produce an accurate tax return. But the process is inefficient, expensive, stressful, and avoidable.

The real tragedy is not that the trucker's records were messy, but rather the money he paid cleaning up the past could have been used to plan for the future.

Instead of spending the client's budget trying to create usable financial reports after the fact, the CPA could be using those reports to help the trucker understand his business. He could help the trucker evaluate fuel costs and understand his operating margins.

The CPA could determine whether certain routes are actually profitable. He could compare the cost of renting, leasing, or purchasing a new truck. He could explain the cash flow impact, tax consequences, depreciation benefits, and long-term financial tradeoffs of each option.

He could help him decide whether it makes sense to continue operating as an LLC or form an S corporation. He could help him set up a 401(k), SEP IRA, or other retirement plan so the business is not just creating income today but building long-term wealth.

He could help him plan estimated tax payments, manage debt, control operating costs, evaluate insurance coverage, build cash reserves, and make better decisions before the money is spent.

These are the conversations that matter. But these conversations rarely happen when the entire accounting budget is consumed by the task of cleaning up records. If the CPA has to spend all his time turning the proverbial "shoebox" into a tax return, there is little time left to help the client understand what the business is doing, where the profits are going, and how the owner can make better decisions.

The goal is not merely to create good financial reports. The financial report should not be the end product. It should be the starting point.

And for the trucker, that could mean lower taxes, better cash flow, a retirement plan, a more profitable business, and long-term wealth.

The new model does not eliminate the accountant.

It elevates him.

Many accountants and business owners mistakenly believe the primary purpose of good accounting is to enable the business owner to timely file an accurate tax return. This is completely backwards.

Saying the primary reason for accounting is to pay taxes is like saying the primary reason for owning a business is to pay vendors. Vendors are necessary. Taxes are necessary. But neither are the purpose of owning a business.

The purpose of a business is to create value, cash flow, build wealth for the owner, and improve the quality of life of the owner and the owner's family. Taxes are simply one of many necessary expenses incurred in the process—no different than rent, payroll, or utilities.

Yet many business owners have been conditioned to believe accounting exists primarily for compliance. Governments reinforce this perspective because governments naturally focus on reporting and tax collection. Traditional accounting systems reinforce it because they are designed around recording history, categorizing transactions, and satisfying reporting requirements.

But business owners do not wake up in the morning excited about categorizing expenses or reconciling bank accounts. They want answers to much more important questions:

Am I making money?

Can I afford to hire?

Should I buy this equipment or lease it?

Why is my cash tight even when sales are increasing?

Am I contributing enough to retirement?

These are life questions. And these questions require financial clarity—not simply bookkeeping compliance.

This is the central idea behind this book. The system itself has become too complicated, time consuming, and disconnected from the actual needs of the owner.

Business owners do not need to become accountants. They need systems, technology, and advisors that translate financial activity into meaningful insight and better forward-looking decisions.

CHAPTER 8

WHAT THIS MEANS FOR ACCOUNTING FIRMS

This is where the conversation usually gets uncomfortable. Because up to this point, everything we've discussed has been focused on the end user. The contractor. The creator. The underserved business owner.

But there is another group at the center of this ecosystem. Accounting firms. And the question they are now facing is not whether accounting is changing, but rather what is their role when it does?

1. Accounting firms did not create this problem. They adapted to it.

They built businesses around maintaining books, cleaning up records, and preparing returns. Because that's what the system required. And for years, that work has been necessary. But it has also been time-consuming, labor-intensive, and difficult to scale. That tension has always been there. Now it's unavoidable.

2. Every firm knows this one truth, even if they don't say it out loud.

A large portion of their time is not spent creating value. It's spent correcting mistakes, chasing documents, reconciling inconsistencies, and rebuilding incomplete records. Work that exists because the system depends on the client to get it right first. And they don't. Not consistently. So, the firm absorbs the cost, time, and frustration.

3. Bookkeeping is the most challenging service you can offer.

Margins are tight. To make it work, firms rely on junior staff, build review layers, and even offshore labor to lower-cost regions. Not because they want to. Because they have to. The work required to maintain the system often exceeds the value the client places on it.

4. Every firm has clients they avoid.

Firms avoid clients who don't keep good records and don't stay organized. Not because they aren't valuable. But because they require too much effort. So, firms avoid them or price them higher. Or take them on reluctantly. Entire segments of the market remain underserved.

5. Growth in a traditional firm is capped.

More clients means more transactions, more cleanup, and more staff. More staff means more management and more overhead. And eventually a ceiling. Growth becomes tied to headcount. And headcount becomes the constraint.

6. From making sausage to showing the sizzle.

If the system no longer requires manual categorization and reconciliation cleanup, then the foundation of the firm shifts. The firm is no longer maintaining the system. It is working with the output. That is not a small change. That is a different model. To put it in marketing speak, the monthly fee for bookkeeping shifts from making sausage to showing the sizzle. In other words, CPAs can use that time to help the business grow and succeed.

7. The new model elevates the accountant.

In the old model: Revenue increases → Labor increases → Margins compress

In the new model: Revenue increases → Labor is stable → Margins grow

This difference is everything. It means more clients and less time spent on chasing missing transactions. Growth is no longer constrained by people. The new model does not eliminate the accountant. It removes the least valuable part of their work. Less time is spent on data entry, categorization, and reconciliation. More time is spent on tax planning and putting money back in the client's pockets. The value of this shift is a no-brainer.

8. The new model serves the underserved.

Remember the clients we talked about earlier. The contractor. The yachtie. The creator. These are not bad clients. They are just incompatible with the current model. But when the system removes the need for manual work, they become valuable. The market expands—without increasing operational strain.

9. Before and after.

Before: Clients maintain their own books inconsistently. Their accountant cleans up and reconstructs. Bookkeeping is labor heavy and low margin. Growth requires hiring. Some clients are avoided.

After: The new model maintains financial data in real time. The accountant works from clean, reliable data. There is less cleanup and more advisory. Growth scales without proportional hiring. Previously "difficult" clients become accessible.

10. The real opportunity is doing meaningful work.

This is not just about efficiency. It's about repositioning. Firms are no longer providers of bookkeeping labor. They become providers of financial clarity and strategic advisors. And that changes their value, which changes pricing.

Accounting firms are not being replaced. They are being redefined. The work that once required constant human effort, no longer does. And once that work is removed, something else becomes possible.

A firm that scales without strain serves more clients and delivers higher value. Not by doing more work, but by doing more *meaningful* work. The future of the accounting firm is not about how efficiently it can maintain books. It's about how effectively it can turn financial data into better decisions.

* * *

A CASE STUDY

THE FIRM PRINCIPAL

Her father had built it up from one desk to a practice that, by the time she took it over in 2008, had 78 clients, 3 staff accountants, and a partner who was three years from retirement. The firm had been in the family since 1971. She had come home to run the company because her father had asked.

For the first twelve years she ran it the way he had. Hourly billing. A hard stop on growth at roughly 100 clients, because more than that and quality would slip. And an informal rule that no one left the office until the last file of the day was clean.

Her partner retired. The staff accountants turned over, as staff accountants do. By 2022, she was the only person at the firm who had been there more than four years.

The moment she describes as "the turning point" was not dramatic. It happened on a Wednesday afternoon in February. One of her young staff accountants—bright, twenty-six— came into her office with a question about how to handle a client's loan receivable.

The question was simple. The staff accountant was not incompetent. But the answer required context that the client had never provided because the client did not think in those terms. The staff accountant had spent the previous six hours trying to reverse-engineer that context from bank statements.

Six hours. One entry. One client.

The following summer she made the change. Not all at once—she migrated 12 clients in the first wave, watched what happened, then moved 20 more in the second. By the end of the year, two-thirds of the book was using the new model.

Her staff no longer spends their afternoons searching for missing entries and now has conversations about what the numbers mean. The billable rate on these conversations are, as it turns out, considerably higher than the billable rate on reconstruction.

Three years later, her headcount is the same. Her client list is three times larger. Her revenue has doubled. She has watched two competing firms consolidate under pressure in the last eighteen months. Her firm is not under pressure.

She is adding clients again, for the first time in almost a decade.

And for the first time in her career, she's not dreading April.

CHAPTER 9

THE ECONOMICS OF THE SHIFT

Why This Change Will Happen

THE OLD EQUATION	THE NEW EQUATION
More Clients	**More Clients**
↓	↓
More Work	**More System Usage**
↓	↓
More People	**Minimal Incremental Cost**
↓	
More Cost	

Revenue tied to labor.	*Revenue decoupled from labor.*
Growth requires hiring.	*Growth driven by system capacity.*
Margins constrained.	*Margins expand with scale.*
Output varies.	*Output consistent.*
Scales slowly.	*Scales quickly.*

One model grows by adding employees. The other grows by adding clients. When two models compete and one of them requires less effort to scale, the winner is obvious.

Every major shift in business follows a predictable pattern. It does not occur because people want it, and it rarely begins with consensus or comfort. Instead, it happens because the economics demand it. Better ideas do not win on their own. Better models do.

And when a model emerges that reduces cost, increases output, and scales more efficiently, it does not simply compete with the existing system—it replaces it.

That is where accounting finds itself today.

For decades, the economics of accounting firms have been built on a straightforward equation. Growth requires more clients. More clients require more work. More work requires more employees. And more employees increase costs. This linear relationship has defined the industry. As firms grow, their margins are continually pressured by the need to add labor, manage staff, and absorb the variability that comes with a human-dependent process.

A significant portion of time is spent not on creating value, but on correcting errors, reclassifying transactions, chasing missing documentation, and reconstructing incomplete records. This work exists because the system relies on the client to maintain accuracy, and in practice, most clients do not. As a result, the firm absorbs the cost of that inconsistency. Time is spent recovering from a lack of structure rather than delivering meaningful insight.

Technology improved access to accounting systems, but it did not change this underlying equation. Software made the process faster and more accessible, but it did not remove the dependency on the business owner. Transactions still needed to be categorized. Accounts still needed to be reconciled. Reports still required validation. The burden shifted slightly, but it did not disappear. In many cases, it simply moved from the firm to the client, and then back again.

The true shift begins when that dependency is removed.

When the system itself performs the classification, structure, and reconciliation of financial data, the economic model changes fundamentally. Growth is no longer tied directly to labor. Instead, it becomes tied to system usage. As more clients enter the system, the incremental cost of serving them declines dramatically. This is where operating leverage emerges.

Operating leverage changes the trajectory of a business. Revenue can grow without a corresponding increase in expenses. Margins expand as scale increases. Output becomes more consistent because it is no longer dependent on varying levels of human input. The firm is no longer constrained by the pace at which it can hire, train, and manage people. Instead, it is enabled by the capacity of the system it has built or adopted.

This shift also changes how services are priced. In the traditional model, pricing is tied to effort. Clients are charged based on hours, tasks, or the complexity of the work required to produce an outcome.

In the new model, pricing is based on outcomes. The outcome, whether due to increased revenues and/or decreased costs, is possible because the business owner can now make more informed decisions. The conversation moves away from how long something took and toward what it is worth.

Speed becomes a defining advantage. In traditional accounting, information is delayed, and decisions are often reactive. By the time financial data is organized and presented, the opportunity to act on it has already passed. In the new model, information is available in real time, allowing for immediate, informed decision-making. The firm that can deliver insight faster than its competitors gains a meaningful advantage.

Over time, these improvements begin to compound. Lower costs lead to higher margins. Higher margins enable greater investment in technology. Better technology attracts more clients and delivers better outcomes. This is the opposite of the traditional model, where growth often introduces complexity and inconsistency.

When viewed side by side, the difference is clear. In the traditional model, revenue is tied directly to labor, growth requires continuous hiring, and margins are constrained by cost. Output varies depending on who performs the work and scalability is limited. In the new model, revenue is decoupled from labor, growth is driven by system capacity, and margins expand as scale increases. Output becomes consistent, and true scalability becomes achievable.

When two models like these exist in the same market, the outcome is not uncertain. One model requires more effort, scales slowly, and produces inconsistent results. The other requires less effort, scales efficiently, and produces consistent outcomes. This is not a matter of preference or opinion. It is a matter of time.

The shift underway in accounting is not driven by desire or tradition. It is driven by economics. And economics does not wait for consensus. It moves steadily and predictably toward efficiency. Once a more efficient model becomes viable, everything around it begins to adjust. The only remaining question is how quickly that adjustment will occur—and who will choose to move with it.

CHAPTER 10

WHY THIS HASN'T HAPPENED SOONER

If the shift described in the previous chapter is as clear and economically compelling as it appears, a reasonable question follows: why hasn't it already happened?

Why does manual accounting still dominate in a world where technology has made much of that work unnecessary? Why do business owners continue to struggle with systems that seem misaligned with how they actually operate? And why have accounting firms not moved more quickly toward a different model?

The answer is not a lack of capability. The tools required to change the system now exist. The constraint has never been innovation alone. It has been a combination of inertia, incentives, and, more recently, the absence of a critical connection between artificial intelligence and real-world expertise.

Every established system carries weight. Over time, processes become embedded not only in software and workflows, but in habits, expectations, and professional identity. Accounting is no exception. The current model is supported by decades of training, certification, and institutional reinforcement. It is taught in universities, tested in professional exams, and practiced daily across firms of every size.

This creates a powerful form of inertia. When a system has worked for a long time, even imperfectly, it becomes the default. Changing that system requires more than a better tool. It requires a willingness to question the assumptions that have supported it.

One of the most persistent of those assumptions is the role of the business owner. Traditional accounting systems are built on the premise that someone must perform the work. Transactions must be entered, categorized, and reconciled by a human being. Even when software simplifies these tasks, it does not remove the expectation that the business owner is responsible for maintaining the system.

That expectation no longer aligns with reality. Business owners operate in environments that are faster, more complex, and more fragmented than ever before. Their financial activity spans multiple platforms, accounts, and income sources.

Yet the system continues to ask them to slow down, organize, and maintain records with a level of consistency that is difficult to sustain. When they fail to meet that expectation, the burden shifts back to the accounting firm, reinforcing the cycle.

Economic incentives further reinforce the status quo. A substantial portion of accounting revenue is derived from work that exists because the system requires maintenance. Bookkeeping, cleanup, reconciliation, and compliance activities all depend on the continuation of manual processes. While many firms recognize that these services are labor-intensive and difficult to scale, they remain predictable sources of revenue.

This creates a difficult trade-off. Moving away from inefficiency requires disrupting not only the client experience, but also the firm's own revenue structure. It introduces short-term uncertainty in exchange for long-term advantage. Not every firm is willing, or positioned, to make that transition quickly.

There is also the matter of trust. Financial systems are inherently sensitive, and both business owners and professionals are cautious about adopting new approaches that affect accuracy, compliance, and reporting. Even when a new model offers clear advantages, it must demonstrate reliability over time. It must prove that it works not only in theory, but consistently, securely, and at scale.

Regulation adds another layer of friction. Accounting and tax operate within frameworks that evolve slowly. These frameworks are designed to ensure consistency and reliability, but they also delay the widespread adoption of new methods. Innovation often moves ahead of formal acceptance, creating a gap between what is possible and what is commonly practiced.

Until recently, there was another limitation as well. The technology required to fully remove the business owner from the process was not sufficiently developed. Software could assist, but it could not replace the underlying work. That has changed with the emergence of accessible artificial intelligence.

AI has created the possibility of automating classification, structure, and interpretation of financial data at a level that was not previously feasible. It has introduced the ability to process large volumes of information quickly and to identify patterns that would be difficult for a human to detect manually.

However, the presence of AI alone does not guarantee better outcomes.

In fact, without proper guidance, it can create new forms of inefficiency.

There is a common assumption that AI, by its nature, produces intelligent results. In practice, the quality of those results depends entirely on how the system is trained, structured, and validated. Without subject matter expertise, AI does not understand context. It processes inputs, but it does not interpret meaning in the way a trained professional does.

Accounting and tax are not purely technical disciplines. They require judgment. They require an understanding of how financial activity translates into reporting obligations, compliance requirements, and business decisions. Without that layer of expertise, automation can produce outputs that appear complete but lack accuracy or relevance.

A simple example illustrates this point:

Consider a Form 1099-B issued by a brokerage firm. Unlike a basic interest statement, this document contains multiple categories of activity within a single report. It may include dividends, interest, short-term transactions with and without cost basis, long-term transactions with and without cost basis, and, in some cases, supplemental adjustments related to employee stock.

From a technical standpoint, it is a single document. From an accounting and tax perspective, it represents multiple distinct reporting elements.

An AI system that has not been trained with subject matter expertise may treat each potential category as a separate output, regardless of whether data exists in each category. The result is not clarity, but fragmentation. A tax preparer may be presented with multiple outputs, many of which contain no relevant information, while the actual reportable data is embedded among them.

In practice, this introduces a new form of risk. The preparer reviews several outputs, sees no activity, and assumes the remaining outputs follow the same pattern. The one output containing meaningful data is easily overlooked. What was intended to improve efficiency instead increases the likelihood of error.

This is not a theoretical problem. It is already occurring in systems that rely heavily on automation without sufficient domain expertise.

The difference between effective and ineffective use of AI in accounting lies not in the technology itself, but in how it is guided. Systems that integrate experienced professionals into their design, testing, and refinement processes produce fundamentally different outcomes than those developed in isolation.

This is why the intersection of artificial intelligence and subject matter expertise represents a turning point. When practicing professionals—those who understand tax law, financial reporting, and business operations—work directly with developers, the system begins to reflect real-world conditions. It produces outputs that align with how financial information is actually used, not just how it is processed.

Many financial technology solutions have been developed primarily by technical teams, often removed from the day-to-day realities of accounting practice and business operations. While these solutions can be functional, they frequently lack the depth required to handle the nuance and variability inherent in financial data.

Bridging that gap requires more than code. It requires continuous interaction between expertise and technology. It requires testing against real scenarios, refining based on actual use, and validating results through professional judgment.

The timing of the current shift is therefore not accidental.

It reflects the moment at which artificial intelligence has become accessible enough to deploy at scale, and subject matter expertise has begun to shape how that intelligence is applied. Only when those two elements intersect does the system begin to function as intended.

Even with this alignment, change does not occur instantly. It begins at the edges, where the existing system is least effective and the cost of maintaining it is highest. It appears first among those who experience the greatest friction, including underserved business owners and firms constrained by capacity.

From there, it expands. As more examples demonstrate success, trust increases. As trust increases, adoption accelerates. What initially appears to be an alternative, gradually becomes the standard.

The delay in this shift is not a sign that it will not occur. It is a reflection of how change unfolds within established systems. It moves through stages of awareness, experimentation, validation, and adoption. Each stage takes time, not because the outcome is uncertain, but because the system itself must adjust.

For business owners, this means that the experience described in earlier chapters may still feel just out of reach, even as it becomes increasingly available. For accounting firms, it means that the opportunity to adapt exists now, but will not remain open indefinitely.

The direction is already set. The only remaining variables are timing and participation. And once the system begins to move, it rarely moves back.

CHAPTER 11

THE DECISION POINT

Every system reaches a moment when continuing forward requires a choice. Not because the old way stopped working, but because a better way now exists. Double-entry accounting did not die. It evolved.

And in that evolution, something fundamental changed: The work moved away from the business owner. What remains is what people always wanted: Clarity. Confidence. Control. The only question left is: Will you keep doing accounting the old way, or will you move beyond it?

Every major shift in business follows the same pattern. It doesn't happen because people want it. It happens because the economics demand it.

And when a new model reduces cost, increases output, and scales more efficiently, it doesn't compete with the old model. It replaces it. That's where accounting is now.

In the old model, pricing is tied to hours and tasks. In the new model, pricing is tied to confidence. The conversation changes from "How long did this take?" to "What is this worth to me?"

In traditional accounting, information is almost always delayed and most decisions are reactive.

In the new model, information is in real-time and decisions are immediate. That speed matters. Not just for the client. For the firm. Because the firm that delivers insight faster, wins.

This shift is not about preference. It's not about tradition. It's not about whether people are ready for it. It is about economics. And economics does not wait. It does not compromise. It does not negotiate. It moves toward efficiency. Always. And once a more efficient model exists...

The only question left is: How long before everything else adjusts to it?

CHAPTER 12

THE CHEESE HAS MOVED

In the late 1990s, *Who Moved My Cheese?* introduced a simple but powerful idea. In the story, cheese represents something of value—security, success, or opportunity—and the characters are forced to confront a moment when that cheese is no longer where it used to be. Some adapt quickly. Others hesitate, hoping things will return to the way they were. The lesson is straightforward: when the environment changes, those who adjust move forward, and those who do not are left behind.

That metaphor has been applied to countless industries, but it is particularly relevant to accounting today.

For accounting professionals, the cheese has moved.

For decades, the value of the profession was tied closely to the work required to maintain financial systems. Recording transactions, categorizing activity, reconciling accounts, and preparing reports were not only necessary tasks, they were also the foundation of the economic model. Firms built processes, staffing structures, and revenue streams around that work. It was stable, predictable, and widely accepted.

That foundation is now shifting.

As systems become capable of performing more of the underlying work, the source of value begins to move away from manual effort and toward guidance. The work that once defined the profession does not disappear, but it becomes less central. In its place, a different set of expectations begins to emerge—expectations centered on clarity, speed, and strategic insight.

This is not a subtle change. It alters how firms operate, how they scale, and how they deliver value to clients. For some professionals, this shift presents an opportunity to evolve. For others, it introduces uncertainty, particularly if their current model depends heavily on the very work that is being reduced.

Adapting to this shift does not require every firm to become a technology company. However, it does require a willingness to engage with the direction the industry is moving. Some firms may choose to build their own internal solutions, leveraging their understanding of client needs and operational workflows. Others may find it more practical to partner with organizations that are already developing and refining these systems in real-world environments. In either case, the decision is less about whether to change and more about how to participate in that change.

The situation is different for small and medium-sized businesses.

For business owners, accounting has been a necessary expense, often accompanied by frustration and inefficiency. The systems they rely on are not central to how they generate income, but they are critical to how they understand and manage it. As a result, the movement of the "cheese" in accounting does not represent a direct threat to their business model.

Instead, it represents an opportunity.

When disruption occurs in a service industry, the impact is not distributed evenly. Those who provide the service may experience pressure to adapt, while those who consume the service often benefit. This pattern has repeated itself across multiple industries.

When Amazon began as an online bookstore, it disrupted the traditional retail model. Over time, that disruption extended far beyond books, affecting a wide range of physical retail businesses. The companies that relied on in-store sales were forced to adapt or compete under new conditions. Consumers, however, benefited from increased convenience, broader selection, and often lower prices.

A similar pattern emerged with Uber and other ride-sharing services. Traditional taxi systems, which operated under a different set of constraints and expectations, faced significant disruption. Consumers, on the other hand, gained access to faster, more flexible, and often more cost-effective transportation options.

In each case, one group experienced the movement of the cheese as disruption, while another experienced it as improvement.

Accounting is following a similar path.

For business owners, the shift toward system-driven financial management has the potential to reduce cost, increase access to timely information, and improve the overall usefulness of that information.

This does not mean that accounting firms that choose not to adopt will fail. Many will continue to operate successfully, particularly in niches with limited competition or in environments where existing processes are sufficient. However, access to accurate, timely, and complete financial information—delivered in a way that is meaningful and usable—can provide a measurable advantage.

Better information leads to better decisions. Better decisions, over time, lead to stronger performance. This advantage may not be immediately visible, but it compounds.

The history of technology adoption offers a useful parallel. Companies that embraced computer systems in the 1980s and 1990s often gained efficiencies that allowed them to operate more effectively than their competitors. Those that delayed adoption were not necessarily eliminated, but they frequently found themselves at a disadvantage in terms of cost, speed, and scalability.

The same dynamic is beginning to take shape in financial systems.

As more businesses gain access to tools that provide real-time clarity and structured insight, the baseline expectation for financial management will rise. What was once considered advanced will become the standard. What was once acceptable may begin to feel insufficient.

Within this evolving landscape, new models are emerging. Some are being developed by technology companies. Others are being shaped by firms that combine professional expertise with system development. In many cases, the most effective solutions are those that integrate both perspectives—leveraging the capabilities of modern technology while remaining grounded in the realities of tax, accounting, and business operations.

This intersection is where meaningful progress tends to occur.

For both accounting professionals and the businesses they serve, the question is not whether to engage with this shift, but how to approach it thoughtfully. The goal is not to adopt new tools for the sake of novelty, but to evaluate whether those tools improve clarity, reduce unnecessary effort, and support better decision-making.

With that in mind, it is useful to step back and consider a few simple questions.

For accounting professionals, the following may be worth reflecting on. How much of your current work is tied to maintaining the books rather than interpreting results? If the manual components of that work were reduced, how would your role change? Are your current processes designed for scale, or are they constrained by the need for additional labor?

And perhaps most importantly, where do you believe the future value of your work will come from?

For business owners, a different set of questions applies. How confident are you in the accuracy and completeness of your financial information at any given time? To what extent does your current system require your time and attention to maintain? How often do you make decisions without having fully up-to-date information? And if a system existed that reduced that burden while improving clarity, how would that affect the way you operate?

These questions are not intended to produce immediate answers. They are intended to encourage reflection.

The purpose of this book has not been to prescribe a single solution, but to highlight a shift that is already underway. That shift is changing how financial systems operate, how accounting professionals deliver value, and how business owners interact with the information that drives their decisions.

The cheese has moved. For some, that movement represents disruption. For others, it represents opportunity. For everyone, it represents change.

CHAPTER 13

WHAT I USUALLY HEAR BACK

Five honest objections with five honest answers

"MY CPA SAYS THE TECHNOLOGY ISN'T READY."

Some of it isn't. Much of it is. The question is not whether every corner of the accounting profession has been fully automated. It hasn't. The question is whether the classification of routine transactions, the reconciliation of bank feeds, and the basic structuring of financial data can be performed by modern systems, without the business owner doing the work manually. They can.

"I DON'T WANT MY FINANCIAL DATA ON SOMEONE ELSE'S SERVER."

That ship sailed when you started using a bank. Your financial data already lives on someone else's server. The only question is whether the server that holds your data can also help you make sense of it. The privacy conversation is real and worth having. It is not specific to tax and accounting. It is a conversation about every piece of software you already use.

"ISN'T THIS JUST LIKE QUICKBOOKS?"

No. QuickBooks, and every product like it, is a place for someone to do accounting. The new model is a place where accounting gets performed on your behalf. The difference sounds small. It is not. One requires you to show up with the discipline of a bookkeeper. The other does not require you to show up at all.

"MY BUSINESS IS TOO COMPLICATED."

All businesses follow patterns. A business that genuinely has no repeating patterns in its financial activity is so rare, that I have not encountered one in thirty years. Most of the people who say this about their business are wrong about their business.

"WHAT HAPPENS TO ACCOUNTANTS?"

The ones who were adding value will continue to add value. The ones who were billing to reconstruct other people's data will either stop, charge for something else, or leave the profession. None of those outcomes are tragedies. Two of them are good for the remaining accountants. All three are good for the people paying the bills.

CHAPTER 14

MONDAY MORNING

There are two readers of this book. One owns a business and has never enjoyed a single interaction with his or her accounting system. The other is in the accounting profession and suspects that something is shifting, but is not sure what, or how fast, or what to do about it. The advice is different for each. What follows is short because the actions should be simple. If they are complicated, they are not the right actions.

* * *

READER A: YOU OWN A BUSINESS

One. Figure out what you are actually paying for.

Pull out your last twelve months of bookkeeping fees, tax-prep fees, cleanup invoices, and the value of whatever time you personally spend on your books. Add it up. Most business owners have never done this. The number is almost always larger than they thought, and a surprising share of it goes to correcting problems that shouldn't exist in the first place.

Two. Ask one question at your next meeting.

The next time you sit down with your accountant, ask: How much of your service is fixing the way my data comes in, versus interpreting what my data means?

Listen carefully to the answer. If most of the work is fixing, you are paying a professional to do clerical recovery. There is a better use of that relationship, and a better use of your money.

Three. Do not replace your accountant. Change what you are asking them for. If they can't do this, then find a new accountant.

A common mistake business owners make after reading a book like this: fire their CPA and buy software. Don't. A capable accountant is one of the most valuable relationships a small business has.

You should change what you are asking them to do. Stop asking them to be the keeper of your books. Start asking them to help you read them. Ask them to help you make better business decisions that will boost revenues and/or decrease costs.

* * *

READER B: YOU ARE AN ACCOUNTANT

One. Look at one client.

Pick a mid-sized client. Not your best, not your worst. For the last twelve months, estimate what % of the hours you billed was spent interpreting their business versus what % was spent cleaning up their data before you could interpret anything. Most firms have never run this number. It is usually worse than the partners believe.

Two. Have the conversation with a partner.

Have the conversation with someone you trust, who will not dismiss your concerns. Ask: what does this client need to know on a regular basis that would help them make better business decisions? What are they constantly calling us about? Where can we save this client money? Focus on the specific outcomes you can deliver beyond just cleaning up their books.

Three. Deliver strategy for one quarter.

Pick one client who is willing. Start reviewing their financial data and delivering personalized insights. Run this for a quarter. Track two things: your hours on that client and the savings you generate for that client. If you generate savings for your client, you can continue testing with this client and/or expand to a second. If you don't, you have learned something. Neither outcome costs the firm its future. Waiting six more months for certainty might.

* * *

READER C: BOTH OF YOU

There is a temptation, after a book like this, to make a decision. To choose something. To commit. That is not what the next week is for.

The next week is for looking honestly at what you already have. The real decision usually makes itself, once you can see what you are actually looking at.

The cheese has moved.

You do not have to move with it today.

You only have to stop pretending it hasn't.

Double-entry accounting is not broken.

It is five hundred years old and still correct.

Every transaction has two sides. It always will.

What has changed is the world around the system.

Transactions were written by hand. Now they are digital, created the moment they happen.

Accounts used to be balanced by candlelight.

Now they can be balanced by a system that does not sleep.

The person using the system used to be a trained bookkeeper.

Now it is a truck driver. A creator. A contractor.

The system hasn't failed.

We just kept asking the wrong person to run it.

Double-entry accounting did not die.

It moved.

From the hand of the business owner...

...into the logic of the system.

Stop doing accounting.

Start running your business.

A FINAL NOTE.

The right system is not the one with the most features, the best marketing, or the lowest price. It is the one that requires the least from you and delivers the most of what you actually need, which is usually something simpler than it sounds: a set of numbers you can trust, on the Monday of any given week.

If it does that, you are finally free from doing accounting.

APPENDIX

QUESTIONS TO ASK BEFORE CHOOSING A SYSTEM

If you are shopping for a new accounting approach—whether it is a software product, a service, or a combination of the two—most of what you will hear from vendors is about features. Features are not the right thing to evaluate. Almost every product now has roughly the same features. What matters is what the product requires from you to deliver those features.

1. How much of this system's work happens without me?

If the answer involves you clicking, approving, or categorizing more than a handful of transactions a week, you are looking at software. You wanted a system.

2. Who is responsible when something goes wrong?

In most software, the answer is you. In a system-first model, it should be someone else. Get that in writing.

3. How do I get my data out?

Every vendor will give you a smooth answer here. Ask for the actual file format. Ask who owns the data in a contract dispute. Ask what happens to your records if the vendor is acquired.

4. What does a bad month look like?

Every system has bad months — data comes in late, a bank changes its feed, a tax authority updates a form. The relevant question is not whether the system has bad months, but what happens during one. Is someone on the line with you, or are you on hold?

5. What does this cost when my business is twice the size?

Pricing that scales linearly with transactions, or linearly with revenue, is pricing designed to extract rent. Pricing that scales with value delivered is pricing designed for a long relationship. Ask for a number at two or three sizes beyond where you are today.

6. Does a human ever look at my books?

There is a version of system-first accounting that is fully automated and a version where a professional reviews the system's work on a regular cadence. The second version is more expensive and usually worth it. Know which one you are buying.

7. What does my CPA think of this?

If you have a CPA you trust, their opinion is usually worth more than the sales pitch. If they dismiss it without looking at it, that is information about your CPA, not about the system. If they look at it carefully and raise specific concerns, listen hard.

* * *

GLOSSARY

Accrual

Recording income when you earn it and expenses when you incur them, regardless of whether the money has actually moved yet. The opposite of cash accounting. Larger or more complicated businesses are on accrual, whether they realize it or not.

Asset

Something the business owns that has value. Cash, inventory, equipment, a building, amounts customers owe you. Assets live on the balance sheet.

Balance Sheet

A snapshot of the business at a moment in time. What you own, what you owe, what is left over. Always balances, by design.

Bookkeeping

The day-to-day recording of financial transactions. Historically the work of a dedicated person. Today, often the work of whoever has the least bandwidth to push back.

Cash Basis

Recording income when money comes in and expenses when money goes out. Simpler than accrual. Less informative. Used by most very small businesses.

Chart of Accounts

The list of categories a business uses to classify its transactions. Every transaction lands somewhere on the chart.

Credit

One side of a transaction. Describes where value came from — what was given up, borrowed, or earned in order to produce the thing on the other side.

Debit

The other side of a transaction. Describes what was received. Not to be confused with the debit on your bank card, which is actually a credit from the bank's point of view. Welcome to accounting.

Double-Entry Accounting

The system, five hundred years old, that says every transaction has two sides and the two must balance. The subject of this book.

Equity

What the owners of the business have left after subtracting what the business owes from what it owns. Also, the number that changes when the business makes or loses money.

Expense

Something the business has spent in the current period that does not create long-term value. Rent, wages, fuel, coffee for the office.

General Ledger

The master record of all transactions, organized by account. Everything eventually flows here.

Income

Money earned through the normal activity of the business. Revenue, sales, fees.

Income Statement (P&L)

A report of what the business made and spent over a period of time. Unlike the balance sheet, it covers a span, not a moment.

Liability

Something the business owes. A loan, a credit card balance, taxes due, a supplier invoice.

Reconciliation

The act of making sure what your books say matches what the outside world says. Most commonly: making the bank balance in your accounting system match the balance on the bank statement.

Revenue

Same as income. Accountants have two words for most things.

Transaction

Any event that affects the financial position of the business. Every transaction has two sides. See double-entry accounting.

www.ingramcontent.com/pod-product-compliance
Lightning Source LLC
LaVergne TN
LVHW022313200926
848481LV00004B/1328

* 9 7 9 8 9 9 6 4 3 1 7 0 0 *